A Benjamin Blog
and his Inquisitive Dog
Guide

England

Anita Ganeri

heinemann raintree

© 2015 Heinemann Raintree
an imprint of Capstone Global Library, LLC
Chicago, Illinois

To contact Capstone Global Library, please
call 800-747-4992, or visit our web site
www.capstonepub.com

Edited by Helen Cox Cannons and Tony Wacholtz
Designed by Steve Mead
Original illustrations © Capstone Global Library
Limited 2015
Illustrated by Sernur ISIK
Picture research by Svetlana Zhurkin
Production by Helen McCreath
Originated by Capstone Global Library Limited

**Library of Congress Cataloging-in-Publication
Data**
Ganeri, Anita, 1961-
  England / Anita Ganeri.
      pages cm.—(Country guides, with Benjamin
Blog and his inquisitive dog)
Includes bibliographical references and index.
ISBN 978-1-4109-9591-9 (pb)
1. England—Juvenile literature. 2. Great Britain—
Juvenile literature. I. Title.
  DA27.5.G356 2015
  942—dc23   2014013420

Printed in the United States of America.
003850

Acknowledgments
We would like to thank the following for permission
to reproduce photographs: Alamy: GL Archive, 7,
Kevin Britland, 14, Michael Kemp, 15; Dreamstime:
Anthony Brown, 17; Getty Images: WireImage/
Matt Kent, 23; Shutterstock: Alison Henley, 22, Bryan
Busovicki, 12, cristapper, 24, Emjay Smith, 11, Filip
Fuxa, 27, Hugh McKean, 19, Ian Woolcock, 13, Jaime
Pharr, 6, JeniFoto, 4, Joe Gough, 20, Jorge Felix
Costa, 9, Kevin Eaves, 10, Kiev.Victor, cover, pdesign,
28, Peteri, 16, Phillip Minnis, 26, 29, Richard Semik, 25,
Stephen Rees, 8, Steve Allen, 18, travellight, 21; XNR
Productions, 5.

Some words are shown in bold, **like this**. You can find
out what they mean by looking in the glossary.

Contents

Welcome to England!

Hello! My name is Benjamin Blog, and this is Barko Polo, my **inquisitive** dog. (He's named after the ancient explorer **Marco Polo**.) We have just returned from our latest adventure— exploring England. We put this book together from some of the blog posts we wrote along the way.

River Tweed

SCOTLAND

Cheviot Hills

Pennine Chain

North Sea

Cumbrian Mountains

Scafell Pike

Lake District

River Ouse

North Yorkshire Dales

Windermere

Irish Sea

Manchester

Peak District

River Trent

The Fens

WALES

River Severn

Birmingham

Great Ouse

River

River Wye

River Thames

N
W   E
S

0   25   50 mi.
0   25   50 km

Bristol

River

London

Salisbury Plain

White Cliffs of Dover

FRANCE

Brighton

Isle of Wight

Seven Sisters

Cornish Riviera

English Channel

Isles of Scilly

BARKO'S BLOG-TASTIC ENGLAND FACTS

England is a small country in western Europe. It is part of the United Kingdom. England has a long coastline, with the Irish Sea on the west and North Sea on the east. On land, it is joined to Scotland in the north and Wales in the west.

5

Historic Places

Posted by: Ben Blog | April 27 at 11:07 a.m.

The first stop on our tour was the fort of Vindolanda on Hadrian's Wall. The wall was built by the Romans to guard the border with Scotland. The Romans invaded England in 43 CE and ruled for more than 350 years. The fort was home for many years to Roman soldiers and their families.

BARKO'S BLOG-TASTIC ENGLAND FACTS

This is King Henry VIII, who ruled England from 1509 to 1547. He is famous for having six wives. His **portrait** hangs in Hampton Court Palace, one of Henry's many homes.

Cousts, Rivers, Lukes, and Moors

From Hadrian's Wall, we headed southwest to Cornwall. It's a **peninsula**—a piece of land that looks like a finger sticking out into the sea. The coast here is amazing, with beautiful beaches and high cliffs. It's a great place for surfing, so I'm off to catch some waves.

I am here!

BARKO'S BLOG-TASTIC ENGLAND FACTS

The longest river that starts and ends in England is the Thames. It flows for 215 miles (346 kilometers) from near Cirencester to the North Sea, passing through London on its way.

We're here in the Lake District, in the northwest of England. It's famous for its lakes and rolling hills. We've already climbed the highest mountain in England—Scafell Pike (3,209 feet, or 978 meters). Now we're off for a boat trip on Windermere, England's longest lake.

BARKO'S BLOG-TASTIC ENGLAND FACTS

Exmoor is a huge stretch of **moorland** in southwest England. It's home to wild Exmoor ponies, red deer, and a legendary black cat called the Beast of Exmoor. Yikes!

City Sights

Posted by: Ben Blog | August 4 at 10:01 a.m.

Our next stop was London, the capital city of England. It's famous for Big Ben, the Tower of London, the British Museum, and lots more. Here's a snapshot of Barko next to one of the soldiers standing guard outside Buckingham Palace, the home of Queen Elizabeth II.

BARKO'S BLOG-TASTIC ENGLAND FACTS

London is a huge place, but not all English cities are as big as this. Wells, in Somerset, is tiny—almost 700 times fewer people live there than in London—but it counts as a city because it has a **cathedral**.

Good Morning!

English is spoken in England and by hundreds of millions of people around the world. It is the main language of countries such as the United States and Australia. A few people in Cornwall speak Cornish, a very ancient language. In Cornish, "good morning" is *myttin da*.

BARKO'S BLOG-TASTIC ENGLAND FACTS

Many people from India, Pakistan, Bangladesh, and the West Indies have come to live in England. They have brought their own languages, beliefs, and traditions with them.

In England, children have to go to school from the ages of four or five to 16. Many children stay in school until they are 18. After school, some students go on to college. Oxford University, in Oxford, is one of the oldest universities in the world.

BARKO'S BLOG-TASTIC ENGLAND FACTS

Many English people live in **suburbs**, just outside towns and cities. Some live in large, modern communities like this one. Some people live in villages in the countryside.

It's Bonfire Night and we're staying in Oxford for a party. Back on November 5, 1605, Guy Fawkes and a group of plotters tried to blow up the Houses of Parliament. Today, people remember this by setting off fireworks and building bonfires with a model of Guy on top.

BARKO'S BLOG-TASTIC ENGLAND FACTS

Many English people are Christians and belong to the Church of England. They worship in churches like this one. But people who have come to live in England have also brought their own religions, such as Islam and Sikhism.

Fish and Chips

Posted by: Ben Blog | March 2 at 12:18 p.m.

We spent the morning sightseeing, then stopped for some fish and chips. ("Chips" are actually French fries.) This meal is very popular in England. Another traditional English meal is Sunday lunch, which has roast meat with potatoes, vegetables, gravy, and sometimes **Yorkshire pudding**.

BARKO'S BLOG-TASTIC ENGLAND FACTS

People who have settled in England have brought their own types of food with them. There are many Indian restaurants serving delicious curries, such as chicken tikka masala (chicken in a spicy sauce).

Anyone for Tennis?

Posted by: Ben Blog | July 1 at 2 p.m.

Back in London, we're watching a tennis match at Wimbledon. Wimbledon is one of the most famous tennis tournaments in the world. It lasts for two weeks in the summer, and players come from all over the world. Wow, what a shot!

BARKO'S BLOG-TASTIC ENGLAND FACTS

The Proms are **classical music** concerts that take place every summer at the Royal Albert Hall in London. There are special Proms for children and families, as well as an open-air Prom in Hyde Park.

From Money to Tourists

Posted by: Ben Blog | September 9 at 8:21 p.m.

London is one of the biggest **financial** centers in the world. It is famous for the Bank of England and the London Stock Exchange. The Bank of England is the second-oldest bank in the world. One of its jobs is to **issue** money and to guard the country's gold reserves.

BARKO'S BLOG-TASTIC ENGLAND FACTS

Millions of tourists visit England each year to see its historic sites, such as Stratford-upon-Avon. This is where William Shakespeare, the famous poet and **playwright**, was born.

And Finally...

For the last stop on our trip, we've come to Salisbury Plain in Wiltshire. We're here to see Stonehenge, the most famous **prehistoric** site in England. The rings of giant stones were probably put up between 2400 and 2200 BCE and were used for religious ceremonies. Amazing!

I am here!

BARKO'S BLOG-TASTIC ENGLAND FACTS
The White Cliffs of Dover in southern England are white because they are made of chalk. From the top, you can get a good view of France, but be careful you don't get too close to the edge!

England Fact File

Area: 50,301 square miles
(130,279 square kilometers)

Population: 53,012,456 (2013)

Capital city: London

Other main cities: Manchester, Birmingham,
   Liverpool

Language: English

Main religion: Christianity

Highest mountain: Scafell Pike
   (3,209 feet/978 meters)

Longest river: Thames (215 miles/346 kilometers)

Currency: Pound sterling

England Quiz

Find out how much you know about England with our quick quiz.

1. Who built Hadrian's Wall?
a) The Anglo-Saxons
b) The Romans
c) King Henry VIII

2. Which is England's largest lake?
a) Windermere
b) Loch Ness
c) Grasmere

3. Who lives in Buckingham Palace?
a) William Shakespeare
b) Queen Elizabeth II
c) The prime minister

4. What sport is played at Wimbledon?
a) basketball
b) soccer
c) tennis

5. What is this?

Answers
1. b
2. a
3. b
4. c
5. Stonehenge

29

Glossary

cathedral large and important church

classical music serious music written by composers and often played by an orchestra

financial relating to finances or money

inquisitive interested in learning about the world

issue send or give out something

Marco Polo explorer who lived from about 1254 to 1324. He traveled from Italy to China.

moorland area of high, open land that is not good for farming

peninsula narrow strip of land sticking out into a body of water

playwright person who writes plays

portrait painting of a person

prehistoric from a time in the past before things were written down

suburb place where people live on the outskirts of a town or city

Yorkshire pudding English dish made from eggs, flour, and milk

Find Out More

Books

Atkinson, Tim. *Discover the United Kingdom* (Discover Countries). New York: PowerKids, 2012.

Burgan, Michael. *United Kingdom in Our World* (Countries in Our World). Mankato, Minn.: Smart Apple Media, 2012.

Throp, Claire. *England* (Countries Around the World). Chicago: Heinemann Library, 2012.

Web sites

Facthound offers a safe, fun way to find Internet sites related to this book. All of the sites on Facthound have been researched by our staff.

Here's all you do:

Visit *www.facthound.com*

Type in this code: 9781410968487

Index